The K‹

Spiritual Warfare through Principles of Dance and Worship

By Susan Michelle Tyrrell, M.A.

Table of Contents

Preface

In the fall of 2008, I taught a class on my passion for worship dance. I had wanted to do some real teaching on it for years, and when I finally had the opportunity, I began to study this subject more intently.

For over ten years, I have been involved in some sort of worship or praise dancing. In 2000, I began taking classes from a ministry called Shachah Ministries International, under the direction of Magrate Yap. Later I went on to dance with Shachah Ministries at Christ for the Nations Women's Conferences and other ministry events, as well as at my own churches in Texas, even leading, however inadequately, dance teams. So I was an expert, right?

Not even close.

Suddenly as I sat down to craft a lesson, I realized I knew a lot but I didn't know how to explain it. Why would anyone, in the middle of a major trial in life, pick up a streamer and dance? That's just weird to the natural mind. And unless I could find the Scriptures for it, it was going to be mighty weird to anyone.

So I studied. I went back to everything I thought I knew and each week sat and plowed through Scriptures. I am not sure I ever studied the Bible as intently as I did during the teaching of this class. But what I gained was invaluable.

First, I learned that even though I called it a class on dance, it wasn't: It was a class on spiritual warfare. That was not a stretch; it was a fact. Additionally, it was a class on the heart of God. It was a class on biblical history. Dance was an expression of these areas, a principle that threads throughout the word of God. I soon realized that in the Bible one thing dance isn't about is dancing for the sake of dancing.

So if you are a dancer, try to read this less as a dance study and more as a Bible study. And if you are not a dancer and think this book is not for you, trust me when I say that isn't necessarily correct. If the Bible is for you, then a book on dance is for you. Really. Even God dances: **"The LORD your God is in your midst, a mighty one who will save; he will rejoice over you with gladness; he will quiet you by his love; he will exult over you with loud singing" (Zep 3:17**) The word exult (joy in KJV) here literally means "to spin around (under the influence of any violent emotion), that is, usually rejoice" *(H1523, Strong's).*

Chapter One

Overview of Scriptural basis for dance

Whoever believes in me,

as the Scripture has said,

"Out of his heart will flow rivers of living water."

-Jesus in John 7:38

*A*nd to the angel of the church in Philadelphia write: The words of the holy one, the true one, who has the key of David, who opens and no one will shut, who shuts and no one opens. I know your works. Behold, I have set before you an open door, which no one is able to shut. I know that you have but little power, and yet you have kept my word and have not denied my name. (Revelation 3:7-8)

I entitled this study *The Key of David* because of this Scripture, and the understanding it gives us of the power of worship and the importance of passionate love for God. David, deemed by the Father Himself as a man after God's own heart, was a man who fell into what we would label "bad" sin. Adultery, murder, lying, all of these made the round of David's life. And yet he was a man God esteemed. Why?

The key of David is his pure worship. Our worship can open doors in the heavenlies; it can also war against those things which we need closed. This book specifically studies the elements of dance as a part of worship and spiritual warfare. Often we don't look at dance as a part of our own spiritual lives if we aren't "dancers." However, the understanding of this form of worship is for anyone: Men, children, ballerinas, even people in wheelchairs. As you read and study this topic, you will see that the principles of dance are applicable to everyone, and when you study the meaning of the words and the context of dance-related worship and warfare in Scripture, there remains no question that this is much more far-reaching than "those people who bounce around during worship."

Opening Doors in Worship Dance

Dance is not the extreme thing it can look like from afar. It's not just for the "wild worshipers." In fact, my own journey with dance began as a grown woman who had had exactly one dance class ever—a miserably failed attempt at ballet, with a blue tutu, in the third grade—and thought that people who danced in worship were only those "weird

Charismatics." I considered myself neither weird nor Charismatic.

I don't want to spend much time focusing on myself in here, but I do want to say that my first real encounter with the power of dance in warfare happened when I saw Psalm 30:18 come to life for me; the Lord literally "turned my mourning into dancing" one Sunday morning in 1998. I walked into church defeated, depressed, and just plain desperate. The worship leader piped in on my morose state with a happy, upbeat victorious song that often caused people to do what my former dance instructor called the "Charismatic Holy Hop." I had never danced in church, thought people who did it were off, and wasn't at all in the "mood."

God had other ideas. Soon the song got into me. I couldn't escape that something spiritual was happening, and while I certainly had every bit of my own will to refuse it, I couldn't think of one good reason to resist a move of God. So, like having a hand extended to me on a dance floor, I stepped up. I don't think anyone knew that in my flowery dress and sling-back black shoes, a real miracle was occurring right there in the middle section. A lot of people were moving. I didn't slip off my shoes or step into an aisle. I was as terrified as I was consumed. But when my feet left the floor, something in me was forever altered. Dramatic statement? Maybe but over a decade later I can still make the same statement about that same day. I understood then what turning mourning into dancing meant. I understood it wasn't simply a pretty metaphor but a literal reality. And that began my quest into dance, not as a form of exercise or entertainment, but as an expression of worship and an element of prayer and spiritual warfare.

It's not about being a dancer—it's about worship. Jesus says in John:

But the hour is coming, and is now here, when the true worshipers will worship the Father in spirit and truth,

for the Father is seeking such people to worship him. God is spirit, and those who worship him must worship in spirit and truth. (John 4:23-24)

Dance is total abandonment. As such, it is an expression of truth. It is almost impossible to hold on to yourself and your will and dance before the Lord. It is like the ultimate surrender because not only do you make a decision of your will to praise, but you have to physically act on that will in such an extreme way that it becomes terribly hard to hold back anything.

Dance is an act of spiritual combat, just as what we normally label as "worship" is. It's an act God encourages, commands, and uses himself.

First let's look at the famous passage on spiritual warfare in the Bible, which we will return to throughout this study. We all know it, but look at it with fresh eyes:

For we do not wrestle against flesh and blood, but against the rulers, against the authorities, against the cosmic powers over this present darkness, against the spiritual forces of evil in the heavenly places. (Ephesians 6:12)

Scripture is clear that we as human beings are not wrestling against forces of other people. Even when a friend betrays us or a person slanders us, more often than not, it's a battle against "cosmic powers." Oh, come on! What about that mean guy who always tells you off? Well, where does his meanness come from? That's certainly not to dismiss our own wills and fleshly messes. We all have them, but Paul is describing those things we *wrestle*, the strongholds, the forces. We spend a lot of time battling things of our own accord. But what does God do?

And every stroke of the appointed staff that the LORD lays on them will be to the sound of tambourines and lyres. Battling with brandished arm, he will fight with them. (Isaiah 30:32)

Wait! Did you just say God fights with tambourines? Like in that old Pentecostal church?

Not quite!

Unfortunately, sometimes our opinion of what we see in the Bible is tainted by what we once saw in church or people we didn't like. If you have ever stood in a service with someone shaking a tambourine off the beat, then probably you can't envision the Genesis 1 God of creation using it as a weapon to bear down on Lucifer himself! But tambourines (also called timbrels) are a key weapon of warfare in the Bible. The kind we used in our dance ministry had a membrane, a hard surface on one side. So when you heard the chorus of tambourines come in the room, it sounded like the march of warfare, not simply a shake-shake-shake. So cut back to that same Genesis 1 God and see what He says. These expressions of worship go back to the Garden of Eden:

Thou hast been in Eden the garden of God; every precious stone was thy covering, the sardius, topaz, and the diamond, the beryl, the onyx, and the jasper, the sapphire, the emerald, and the carbuncle, and gold: the workmanship of thy tabrets and of thy pipes was prepared in thee in the day that thou wast created. (Ezekiel 28:13-KJV)

God created even the tabret (timbrel or tambourine-*Strong's H8596*) for worship in the Garden of Eden. A timbrel is one of the oldest forms of a worship tool in existence and is used throughout the Bible in tandem with dance.

Dance literally can undo the work of the enemy. One of my dance leaders would teach us that when we spin it is like we are undoing what the devil has done—in a way, it is a willful sacrifice of praise in the midst of whatever assails us that would, in effect, do just that. The enemy would desire us to give in, to take a victim mentality... we can't do anything for God because [insert non-applicable reason here]. To dance is an act of rising in the midst of pain and saying "I *will* rejoice." See these examples:

I appeal to you therefore, brothers, by the mercies of God, to present your bodies as a living sacrifice, holy and acceptable to God, which is your spiritual worship. (Romans 12:1)

And he put all things under his feet and gave him as head over all things to the church (Ephesians 1:22)

Rejoice in the Lord always; again I will say, Rejoice. (Philippians 4:4)

There is also an act of warfare even in waving banners. Sometimes when we dance, it is as if the streamers or flags are being flung at the enemy. Our enemies are spiritual and exist in heavenly places (Ephesians 6:12). The lack of our ability to see them physically doesn't in any way diminish their reality. But the enemy likely enjoys the fact we can't fathom these spiritual oppositions because he gets away with more. When we fling and wave and war and move, any demon is "slapped" continually. Just as a human will duck when something comes at him, how much more will an enemy of our soul, whom we continually battle? Eventually it would make someone leave the "line of fire." When we do that as worship and warfare, that is what happens to the enemy in the spiritual realm.

Passivity is an invitation to the enemy. The enemy can pounce on passivity in our lives. When we sit back and take the blows dealt us but don't rise up and act, he has an open door (Ephesians 6:12-18). We are to take an active role in our spiritual life and vibrancy. Physical acts are biblical expressions of worship in this manner.

Foundations of Dance: Worship is Worship

There should be no distinction in a spiritual sense between worshiping and dancing (or singing, clapping, marching, etc). They are all subtypes of worship.

We worship because we are commanded to worship God

Psa 29:2 - Give unto the Lord the glory due to His name; Worship the Lord in the beauty of holiness.

Psa 45:11 - So the King will greatly desire your beauty; Because He is your Lord, worship Him.

Psa 95:6 - Oh come, let us worship and bow down; Let us kneel before the Lord our Maker.

Psa 96:9 - Oh, worship the Lord in the beauty of holiness! Tremble before Him, all the earth.

Psa 99:5 - Exalt the LORD our God; worship at his footstool! Holy is he!

We worship because it brings truth that sets people free

John 4:23 - But the hour is coming, and now is, when the true worshipers will worship the Father in spirit and truth; for the Father is seeking such to worship Him.

John 4:24 - God is Spirit, and those who worship Him must worship in spirit and truth."

1 Co 14:25 - And thus the secrets of his heart are revealed; and so, falling down on his face, he will worship God and report that God is truly among you.

We worship because it is our calling for eternity

Rev 4:10-11 - The twenty-four elders fall down before Him who sits on the throne and worship Him who lives forever and ever, and cast their crowns before the throne, saying, "Worthy are you, our Lord and God, to receive glory and honor and power, for you created all things, and by your will they existed and were created."

Rev 15:4 - Who shall not fear You, O Lord, and glorify Your name? For You alone are holy. For all nations shall come and worship before You, For Your judgments have been manifested."

Rev 19:10 - And I fell at his feet to worship him. But he said to me, "See that you do not do that! I am your fellow servant, and of your brethren who have the testimony of Jesus. Worship God! For the testimony of Jesus is the spirit of prophecy."

<u>We worship Him prophetically, believing for the nations to come to Him</u>

Psa 22:27 - All the ends of the earth shall remember and turn to the LORD, and all the families of the nations shall worship before you.

Psa 22:29 - All the prosperous of the earth eat and worship; before him shall bow all who go down to the dust, even the one who could not keep himself alive.

Psa 66:4 - All the earth shall worship You And sing praises to You; They shall sing praises to Your name.

Psa 86:9 - All nations whom You have made Shall come and worship before You, O Lord, And shall glorify Your name.

Isa 66:23 - And it shall come to pass That from one New Moon to another, And from one Sabbath to another, All flesh shall come to worship before Me," says the Lord.

<u>We worship the one true God while others trust in others gods or themselves</u>

John 4:22 - You worship what you do not know; we know what we worship, for salvation is of the Jews.

Phil 3:3 - For we are the circumcision, who worship God in the Spirit, rejoice in Christ Jesus, and have no confidence in the flesh

Psa 20:7 - Some trust in chariots and some in horses, but we trust in the name of the LORD our God.

Dance and Worship

<u>We dance because God said we should—it is a part of normal worship</u>

Psa 149:3 - Let them praise His name with the dance; Let them sing praises to Him with the timbrel and harp.

Psa 150:4 - Praise Him with the timbrel and dance; Praise Him with stringed instruments and flutes!

Rom 12:1- I beseech you therefore, brethren, by the mercies of God, that you present your bodies a living sacrifice, holy, acceptable to God, which is your reasonable service.

We dance because it is time to let go of our hurt and mourning

Ecc 3:4 - A time to weep, And a time to laugh; A time to mourn, And a time to dance.

Psa 30:8- Weeping may endure for a night, but joy comes in the morning.

Jer 31:13 - Then shall the virgin rejoice in the dance, And the young men and the old, together; For I will turn their mourning to joy, Will comfort them, And make them rejoice rather than sorrow.

We dance with flags because it demonstrates God and His truth in our lives

Psa 60:4 - You have given a banner to those who fear You, That it may be displayed because of the truth.

We raise our banners because God uses this to draw people to Himself

Isa 5:26 - He will lift up a banner to the nations from afar, And will whistle to them from the of the earth; Surely they shall come with speed, swiftly.

We raise our banners in dance as a symbol of raising Jesus to people so they will come to Him

Isa 11:10 - And in that day there shall be a Root of Jesse, Who shall stand as a banner to the people; For the Gentiles shall seek Him, And His resting place shall be glorious.

John 12:32 And I, when I am lifted up from the earth, will draw all people to myself.

<u>We dance with flags because God tells us to so we can call others to Him</u>

Isa 13:2 - Lift up a banner on the high mountain, Raise your voice to them; Wave your hand, that they may enter the gates of the nobles.

<u>We dance with flags and banners because it builds up the kingdom of God and breaks down the things that do not belong in us</u>

Isa 62:10 - Go through, Go through the gates! Prepare the way for the people; Build up, Build up the highway! Take out the stones, Lift up a banner for the peoples!

<u>We raise our banners to show the victory the Lord has given to us</u>

Zec 9:16 - The Lord their God will save them in that day, As the flock of His people. For they shall be like the jewels of a crown, Lifted like a banner over His land—

<u>We raise our banners to fight the devil just as God does</u>

Jer 51:12 - Set up the standard upon the walls of Babylon, make the watch strong, set up the watchmen, prepare the ambushes: for the LORD hath both devised and done that which he spake against the inhabitants of Babylon.

Isa 59:19 - So shall they fear the name of the LORD from the west, and his glory from the rising of the sun. When the enemy shall come in like a flood, the Spirit of the LORD shall lift up a standard against him.

The Word says that God, Himself, raises up a standard against the enemy. We are also admonished to raise up a standard. That word in the Bible is literally a flag. Think about the symbolism of flags in the world. We wave flags in relation to wars. After September 11, many people had flags attached to their cars or homes. They were saying, "the enemy has attacked, but I am raising up a standard stronger than that." But we go into church, often churches that have flags hanging *in* them, and we stand there not giving thought to what it means.

Flags are a symbol of power and victory—even of superiority. God is saying to raise up the standard, the flag, as a way of waving it over the enemy and the defeats in our lives; we do this by declaring a spiritual victory.

I will never forget when I knew of a church forbidding flags because they were too distracting. It broke my heart because I was teaching at a high school at the time, and the students were in tryouts for the color guard. Kids were carrying around flags all the time. The schools were raising flags as a sign of victory over a game but churches were afraid to take up that aspect. We have to raise our symbols of victory.

<u>Worship is a Lifestyle</u>

In Revelation 2-3, the seven churches Jesus addresses display a prophetic picture of the church. While many interpret Revelation all symbolically, much of it is very literal; the symbolism is clearly stated as such. These churches are a picture for us to view the church. These are not letters to unbelievers, but to us. Mike Bickle, Director of the International House of Prayer in Kansas City, summarizes the admonition of each of these letters in his notes on these churches:

To the church of Ephesus overcoming meant to return to their first love for Jesus until the end of their life. To the church in Smyrna it meant being faithful in persecution even to death. To the church in Pergamos and Thyatira overcoming meant to resist immorality and idolatry for the remainder of their life. To the church in Sardis it was be watchful or to develop a prayer life and to hold fast the things that God entrusted to them from their earlier years. To the church in Philadelphia overcoming meant to persevere in mature obedience for the remaining years of their life. To the church of the Laodiceans overcoming meant to resist lukewarmness. (Bickle, "The Seven Churches of Revelation," 5).

Even the church Jesus expresses is living right is admonished it must continue. To not persevere, to not fight, is to fall back. Many of the churches (read: Christians) rely on works or **"having the appearance of godliness, but denying its power. Avoid such people." (2Timothy 3:5)**

Visual Worship as a Sign to "Seekers"

Our church society in the Western world has become very much a "seeker driven" society, even in the Charismatic and Pentecostal churches. Many leaders are afraid their people will be turned off or that visitors will be "freaked out," or otherwise driven from the church if they don't understand what is going on. I believe the answer to this accusation is stated by Jesus Himself:

But the hour is coming, and is now here, when the true worshipers will worship the Father in spirit and truth, for the Father is seeking such people to worship him. God is spirit, and those who worship him must worship in spirit and truth. (John 4:23-24)

And I, when I am lifted up from the earth, will draw all people to myself. (John 12:32)

The bottom line, whether it's worship as we traditionally view it, such as singing and instruments, or if it's more visual, dancing, painting, sacred artistry of all types, is that if it glorifies Jesus, He will be lifted up. Truth will come forth and, in His words:

You will know the truth and the Truth will make you free. (John 8:32)

Chapter Two

Dancing as warfare

The words of the holy one, the true one who has the key of David, who opens and no one will shut who shuts and no one opens.

-Jesus in Revelation 3:7

The Bible absolutely sets a precedent for the normal Christian life being one of warfare.

But if it makes no peace with you, but makes war against you, then you shall besiege it. (13) And when the LORD your God gives it into your hand, you shall put all its males to the sword, (14) but the women and the little ones, the livestock, and everything else in the city, all its spoil, you shall take as plunder for yourselves. And you shall enjoy the spoil of your enemies, which the LORD your God has given you. (Deuteronomy 20:12-14)

Ecc 3:4, 8 - a time to weep, and a time to laugh; a time to mourn, and a time to dance; (8) a time to love, and a time to hate; a time for war, and a time for peace.

Neh 4:20 - In the place where you hear the sound of the trumpet, rally to us there. Our God will fight for us.

Exo 15:3 - The LORD is a man of war; the LORD is his name.

Psa 18:34 - He trains my hands for war, so that my arms can bend a bow of bronze.

Num 10:9 - And when you go to war in your land against the adversary who oppresses you, then you shall sound an alarm with the trumpets, that you may be remembered before the LORD your God, and you shall be saved from your enemies.

Spiritual warfare is a mandate from God for the normal Christian. Again, Ephesians 6:11-18 sets this standard:

Put on the whole armor of God, that you may be able to stand against the schemes of the devil. (Ephesians 6:11)

Put on means action on our part; the statement itself is a command to action. We have to put it on by our own will. It never says "While you stand there doing nothing, God will put on your armor." He gives us the tools but it is our responsibility to step out and use them.

As we noted in chapter one, passivity is an invitation to the enemy: The enemy can pounce on passivity in our lives. When we sit back and take the blows dealt us but don't rise up and act, he has an open door. (Ephesians 6:12-18). We are to take an active role in our spiritual life and vibrancy. Physical acts are biblical expressions of worship in this manner.

Jesus loves us, but Satan hates us; he rages against us and wars whether we do or not. While that is a harsh statement, it's also the truth. Satan doesn't relax his grip—he and his demons don't go, "Oh, Sue's a bit worn out with the stress of life today, so I think I will give her a break." On the contrary, he looks for a way in, and our inactivity will give him a door. James 4:7 says, **Submit yourselves therefore to God. Resist the devil, and he will flee from you.** The Greek word for resist *(Strong's G436)* is the same meaning as the common dictionary definitions. It's an active verb:

a. *to withstand, strive against, or oppose: to resist infection; to resist temptation.*

b. *to withstand the action or effect of: to resist spoilage.*

c. *to refrain or abstain from, esp. with difficulty or reluctance:*

–verb (used without object)

d. *to make a stand or make efforts in opposition; act in opposition; offer resistance.*

–noun

e. *a substance that prevents or inhibits some effect from taking place, (source: resist. (n.d.). Dictionary.com Unabridged (v 1.1).*

Retrieved September 13, 2008, from Dictionary.com website: http://dictionary.reference.com/browse/resist)

One of the most elementary laws of physics states that for each and every action there is an equal and opposite reaction. This basic law of physics parallels the kingdom of God versus the natural world. The natural and supernatural worlds are opposites. In 2 Corinthians 12:1-9, Paul lays the foundation for this with his thorn in the side.

But he said to me, "My grace is sufficient for you, for my power is made perfect in weakness." Therefore I will boast all the more gladly of my weaknesses, so that the power of Christ may rest upon me. (2 Corinthians 12:9)

For though we walk in the flesh, we are not waging war according to the flesh. (4) For the weapons of our warfare are not of the flesh but have divine power to destroy strongholds. (5) We destroy arguments and every lofty opinion raised against the knowledge of God, and take every thought captive to obey Christ, (6) being ready to punish every disobedience, when your obedience is complete. (2 Corinthians 10:3-6)

This may seem extreme, fighting real battles with spiritual weapons we can't see, and yet God has consistently demonstrated that the real fight is spiritual. It's entirely illogical that a literal wall could crumble by marching such as God instructs in Joshua:

You shall march around the city, all the men of war going around the city once. Thus shall you do for six days (4) Seven priests shall bear seven trumpets of rams' horns before the ark. On the seventh day you shall march around the city seven times, and the priests shall blow the trumpets. (5)And when they make a long blast with the ram's horn, when you hear the sound of the trumpet, then all the people shall shout with a great shout, and the wall of the city will fall down flat, and the people shall go up, everyone straight before him." (Joshua 6:3-5)

The Strong's Hebrew word for march used here:

H5437 sâbab: *to revolve, surround or border; used in various applications, literally and figuratively: - bring, cast, fetch, lead, make, walk, whirl, round about, be about on every side, apply, avoid, beset (about), besiege, bring again, carry (about), change, cause to come about, circuit, compass (about, round), drive, environ, on every side, beset (close, come, compass, go, stand) round about, remove, return, set, sit down, turn (self) (about, aside, away, back).*

Jesus' own death and resurrection were the ultimate physical acts of spiritual warfare:

And you, who were dead in your trespasses and the uncircumcision of your flesh, God made alive together with him, having forgiven us all our trespasses, (14) by canceling the record of debt that stood against us with its legal demands. This he set aside, nailing it to the cross. (15) He disarmed the rulers and authorities and put them to open shame, by triumphing over them in him. (Colossians 2:13-15)

But when Christ had offered for all time a single sacrifice for sins, he sat down at the right hand of God. (Hebrews 10:12)

No physical tool can overpower the power of God in warring against darkness.

The war horse is a false hope for salvation, and by its great might it cannot rescue. (Psalm 33:17)

Dance is a powerful tool in spiritual warfare

Again, dance is an act of spiritual combat, just as worship is. It's an act God encourages, commands and uses Himself. It's simply offering the body in a sacrifice of praise. Again, we look at some of the key foundations for the acts of spiritual warfare.

For we do not wrestle against flesh and blood, but against the rulers, against the authorities, against the cosmic

powers over this present darkness, against the spiritual forces of evil in the heavenly places. (Ephesians 6:12)

And every stroke of the appointed staff that the LORD lays on them will be to the sound of tambourines and lyres. Battling with brandished arm, he will fight with them. (Isaiah 30:32)

<u>Dancers and worshipers have always been on the frontlines</u>

And when he had taken counsel with the people, he appointed those who were to sing to the LORD and praise him in holy attire, as they went before the army, and say, "Give thanks to the LORD, for his steadfast love endures forever. (2 Chronicles 20:21)

Dancing is more than the "Charismatic Holy Hop" or a fluid ballet. Warring dance isn't always pretty but the words associated most commonly with them mean both dance and war all at once.

One common Strong's word associated with dance and its meaning has some stark images:

H2342 chûl/chîyl: to twist or whirl (in a circular or spiral manner), that is, (specifically) to dance, to writhe in pain or fear; figuratively to wait, to pervert: - bear, (make to) bring forth, (make to) calve, dance, drive away, fall grievously (with pain), fear, form, great, grieve, (be) grievous, hope, look, make, be in pain, be much (sore) pained, rest, shake, shapen, (be) sorrow (-ful), stay, tarry, travail (with pain), tremble, trust, wait carefully (patiently), be wounded.

This word is one most often associated with warfare in dance and can be found throughout the Old Testament to refer to travail, pain, intercession and other related areas. In other words, dance doesn't mean just "dance" in literal terms; it means travail in pain and war.

<u>Literal vs. figurative speech in the Bible</u>

Even if it seems symbolic, it isn't always. There are powers of wickedness in heavenly places in the air around us. This isn't just a "Christian way of thinking." Warring in the dance is not just a symbolic act. While it can have an element of symbolism, we have to remember the spiritual world is a literal word, and the very stomping of our feet if our spirits are aligned with His, might literally stomp on the Kingdom of darkness.

1Sa 17:20 - And David rose early in the morning and left the sheep with a keeper and took the provisions and went, as Jesse had commanded him. And he came to the encampment as the host was going out to the battle line, shouting the war cry.

Psa 144:1 - Blessed be the LORD, my rock, who trains my hands for war, and my fingers for battle.

Isa 42:13 - The LORD goes out like a mighty man, like a man of war he stirs up his zeal; he cries out, he shouts aloud, he shows himself mighty against his foes.

Heb 11:32-34 - And what more shall I say? For time would fail me to tell of Gideon, Barak, Samson, Jephthah, of David and Samuel and the prophets-- who through faith conquered kingdoms, enforced justice, obtained promises, stopped the mouths of lions, quenched the power of fire, escaped the edge of the sword, were made strong out of weakness, became mighty in war, put foreign armies to flight.

Feet matter! Stop for a minute and picture a group of soldiers, and then imagine them doing their jobs of defending our soil without feet. Ludicrous, right? I have known people not allowed to join a branch of the military for reasons such as having a certain kind of metal plate in a leg from a surgery. Yet we enter spiritual combat with spiritual metal plates. We march without feet. God clearly creates a theme of the power of using feet in spiritual warfare:

Jos 10:24 - And when they brought those kings out to Joshua, Joshua summoned all the men of Israel and said to the chiefs of the men of war who had gone with him, "Come near; put your feet on the necks of these kings." Then they came near and put their feet on their necks.

Jos - 14:9 And Moses swore on that day, saying, 'Surely the land on which your foot has trodden shall be an inheritance for you and your children forever, because you have wholly followed the LORD my God.'

Mal 4:3 - And you shall tread down the wicked, for they will be ashes under the soles of your feet, on the day when I act, says the LORD of hosts.

Rom 16:20 - The God of peace will soon crush Satan under your feet. The grace of our Lord Jesus Christ be with you.

1Co 15:25 - For he must reign until he has put all his enemies under his feet. (26) The last enemy to be destroyed is death.

Eph 6:14-15 - Stand therefore, having fastened on the belt of truth, and having put on the breastplate of righteousness, (15) and, as shoes for your feet, having put on the readiness given by the gospel of peace.

God's precedent for spiritual warfare is also His prophecy for the end times. When Jesus returns to establish His Kingdom on earth, it will be a literal war.

Also it was allowed to make war on the saints and to conquer them. And authority was given it over every tribe and people and language and nation, (8) and all who dwell on earth will worship it, everyone whose name has not been written before the foundation of the world in the book of life of the Lamb who was slain. (9) If anyone has an ear, let him hear: (10) If anyone is to be taken captive, to captivity he goes; if anyone is to be slain with the sword, with the sword must he be slain. Here is a call for the endurance and faith of the saints. (Rev. 13: 7-10)

Then I saw heaven opened, and behold, a white horse! The one sitting on it is called Faithful and True, and in righteousness he judges and makes war. (Rev. 19:11)

It's easy for us to look at the prophecy of Revelation and say, yes, but that is the end of the age, and Jesus will come back; we already know in the end we win.

We can win now, too! Jesus is here in the power of the Holy Spirit. 1 John 4:4 says: **Little children, you are from God and have overcome them, for he who is in you is greater than he who is in the world.** When we choose to put on the garments of praise, use the spiritual weapons of our warfare, tread upon the feet of the enemy, and otherwise war in the present, we are winning the war. We are opening and shutting doors *now*. We do not have to wait for Jesus to return because He has given us power and authority to wage war against the enemy of our soul now. It's our privilege— and duty—to plunder the darkness:

Mat 12:29 - Or how can someone enter a strong man's house and plunder his goods, unless he first binds the strong man? Then indeed he may plunder his house.

Mat 16:19 - "I will give you the keys of the kingdom of heaven, and whatever you bind on earth shall be bound in heaven, and whatever you loose on earth shall be loosed in heaven."

John 14:12 - "Truly, truly, I say to you, whoever believes in me will also do the works that I do; and greater works than these will he do, because I am going to the Father."

Few Bible scholars would argue that times will get harder in the natural sense as we near the coming of Christ. Most agree we have entered the "beginning of birth pains" (see Matthew 24), which in themselves will be a difficult season. If it's very likely we are in this season now, we must be prepared to war against the darkness. But we also must remember that David had the key when he said:

Though an army encamp against me, my heart shall not fear; though war arise against me, yet I will be confident. (Psalm 27:3)

Psalm 149 always strikes me with its commands to dance and war. Read it closely without the "verse breaks":

Praise the LORD! Sing to the LORD a new song, his praise in the assembly of the godly! Let Israel be glad in his Maker; let the children of Zion rejoice in their King! Let them praise his name with dancing, making melody to him with tambourine and lyre! For the LORD takes pleasure in his people; he adorns the humble with salvation. Let the godly exult in glory; let them sing for joy on their beds. Let the high praises of God be in their throats and two-edged swords in their hands, to execute vengeance on the nations and punishments on the peoples, to bind their kings with chains and their nobles with fetters of iron, to execute on them the judgment written! This is honor for all his godly ones. Praise the LORD!

This Psalm alone is reason enough to war and fight in dance. It speaks of the believer's spiritual authority to execute judgment on nations, with no separation from dancing and praise. That is because they are absolutely intertwined. God isn't some cranky man in the sky who is angry for no reason. God is righteous and whatever stands against Him is coming against the righteousness of who He is. Therefore, to have this type of worship separate from godly warfare would be plain old anger. God isn't angry. In fact, it says in Hebrews 1:19: **You have loved righteousness and hated wickedness; therefore God, your God, has anointed you with the oil of gladness beyond your companions.** Jesus was the most joyful man who ever lived, yet we see in Revelation that He will execute kings, that He will literally make war to bring peace. The reason for this is the honor and worship of the truth, of Jesus Christ. Anger apart from righteousness, which is part of worship, is not anger God ordains. Thus, our battles are battles of worship, not of fighting for the sake of a boxing match.

Chapter Three

Tools of worship and why they matter

You are beautiful as Tirzah, my love,

lovely as Jerusalem

awesome as an army with banners.

-Song of Solomon 6:4

As we saw in Psalm 149, and many passages before it, often in warfare, there are various tools used: tambourines and flags (also called standards, which we also know as streamers or ribbons), tassels, and glory hoops, among others. Whatever the name, the point is the same in the worship sense. They are tools used to heighten worship and proclaim or declare the word of the Lord. Clearly a piece of fabric held up high has no innate power, but there is a spiritual—and actually even a natural—connection to this and why it is right and appropriate. It's clear that the Bible shows us a definite connection between the use of banners (which includes flags, streamers, etc) and active, armed warfare.

And when he had taken counsel with the people, he appointed those who were to sing to the LORD and praise him in holy attire, as they went before the army, and say, "Give thanks to the LORD, for his steadfast love endures forever." (2 Chronicles 20:21)

You are beautiful as Tirzah, my love, lovely as Jerusalem, awesome as an army with banners. (Song of Solomon 6:4)

And every stroke of the appointed staff that the LORD lays on them will be to the sound of tambourines and lyres. Battling with brandished arm, he will fight with them. (Isaiah 30:32)

Continually, throughout the Bible, God parallels banners, flags, even Levitical attire, with spiritual warfare, as well as with worship:

Psa 60:4 - You have set up a banner for those who fear you, that they may flee to it from the bow.

Psa 20:5 - May we shout for joy over your salvation, and in the name of our God set up our banners! May the LORD fulfill all your petitions!

Son 2:4 - He brought me to the banqueting house, and his banner over me was love.

Son 6:10 - "Who is this who looks down like the dawn, beautiful as the moon, bright as the sun, awesome as an army with banners?"

 Isa 5:26 - He will lift up a banner to the nations from afar, And will whistle to them from the end of the earth; Surely they shall come with speed, swiftly.

Isa 11:10 - "And in that day there shall be a Root of Jesse, Who shall stand as a banner to the people; For the Gentiles shall seek Him, And His resting place shall be glorious."

 Isa 13:2 - "Lift up a banner on the high mountain, Raise your voice to them; Wave your hand, that they may enter the gates of the nobles.

Isa 59:19 - So shall they fear the name of the LORD from the west, and his glory from the rising of the sun. When the enemy shall come in like a flood, the Spirit of the LORD shall lift up a standard against him.

Isa 62:10 - Go through, Go through the gates! Prepare the way for the people; Build up, Build up the highway! Take out the stones, Lift up a banner for the peoples!

Jer 4:6- Raise a standard toward Zion, flee for safety, stay not, for I bring disaster from the north, and great destruction.

Jer 4:21 - How long must I see the standard and hear the sound of the trumpet?

Jer 50:1-3 - The word that the LORD spoke concerning Babylon, concerning the land of the Chaldeans, by Jeremiah the prophet: "Declare among the nations and proclaim, set up a banner and proclaim, conceal it not, and say: 'Babylon is taken, Bel is put to shame, Merodach is dismayed. Her images are put to shame, her idols are dismayed.' "For out of the north a nation has come up against her, which shall make her land a desolation, and none shall dwell in it; both man and beast shall flee away."

Jer 51:12 - Set up a standard against the walls of Babylon; make the watch strong; set up watchmen; prepare the ambushes; for the LORD has both planned and done what he spoke concerning the inhabitants of Babylon.

Jer 51:27 - Set up a standard on the earth; blow the trumpet among the nations; prepare the nations for war against her; summon against her the kingdoms, Ararat, Minni, and Ashkenaz; appoint a marshal against her; bring up horses like bristling locusts.

Zec 9:16 - The Lord their God will save them in that day, As the flock of His people. For they shall be like the jewels of a crown, Lifted like a banner over His land—

The Lord our Banner

The Lord is literally our banner. Moses demonstrates this in Exodus, which is the reference to *Jehovah Nissi*, which means, the Lord our banner.

And Moses built an altar and called the name of it, The LORD Is My Banner, saying, "A hand upon the throne of the LORD! The LORD will have war with Amalek from generation to generation." (Exodus 17:15-16)

The Sons of Israel were commanded to set up their camps by their standards for each tribe and family. The tribes of Israel are pivotal to the worship of God and are some of the early people to use flags in their worship. The Strong's word mentioned below is *H1714 (degel), from H1713; a flag: - banner, standard.* Watch the pattern and note the precision of the instruction:

Num 2:2 - The people of Israel shall camp each by his own standard, with the banners of their fathers' houses. They shall camp facing the tent of meeting on every side.

Num 2:3 - Those to camp on the east side toward the sunrise shall be of the standard of the camp of Judah by their companies, the chief of the people of Judah being Nahshon the son of Amminadab,

Num 2:10 - On the south side shall be the standard of the camp of Reuben by their companies, the chief of the people of Reuben being Elizur the son of Shedeur,

Num 2:17 - Then the tent of meeting shall set out, with the camp of the Levites in the midst of the camps; as they camp, so shall they set out, each in position, standard by standard.

Num 2:18 - On the west side shall be the standard of the camp of Ephraim by their companies, the chief of the people of Ephraim being Elishama the son of Ammihud,

Num 2:25 - On the north side shall be the standard of the camp of Dan by their companies, the chief of the people of Dan being Ahiezer the son of Ammishaddai,

Num 2:31 - All those listed of the camp of Dan were 157,600. They shall set out last, standard by standard.

Num 2:34 - Thus did the people of Israel. According to all that the LORD commanded Moses, so they camped by their standards, and so they set out, each one in his clan, according to his fathers' house.

Num 10:9 - And when you go to war in your land against the adversary who oppresses you, then you shall sound an alarm with the trumpets, that you may be remembered before the LORD your God, and you shall be saved from your enemies.

Again, because God's precedent for spiritual warfare is also His prophecy for the end times, when the Kingdom of Heaven is established on earth, there will be an actual war. We have every reason to believe that if there are banners in warfare and worship throughout time thus far, this will not cease in the end times.

In Revelation, we see the tribes listed, as they stand before the Lamb of God waving palm branches, again a type of "standard":

And I heard the number of the sealed, 144,000, sealed from every tribe of the sons of Israel: (5)12,000 from the

tribe of Judah were sealed, 12,000 from the tribe of Reuben, 12,000 from the tribe of Gad, (6) 12,000 from the tribe of Asher, 12,000 from the tribe of Naphtali, 12,000 from the tribe of Manasseh, (7) 12,000 from the tribe of Simeon, 12,000 from the tribe of Levi, 12,000 from the tribe of Issachar, (8) 12,000 from the tribe of Zebulun, 12,000 from the tribe of Joseph, 12,000 from the tribe of Benjamin were sealed. (9) After this I looked, and behold, a great multitude that no one could number, from every nation, from all tribes and peoples and languages, standing before the throne and before the Lamb, clothed in white robes, with palm branches in their hands, (10) and crying out with a loud voice, "Salvation belongs to our God who sits on the throne, and to the Lamb!" (11) And all the angels were standing around the throne and around the elders and the four living creatures, and they fell on their faces before the throne and worshiped God, (12) saying, "Amen! Blessing and glory and wisdom and thanksgiving and honor and power and might be to our God forever and ever! Amen." (Revelation 7:4-12)

The prophecy of Revelation isn't just for the end of this age. As we see from thousands of years before, God prepares. He has us set up our flags, our warfare, and our tools to fight. He prepares us far ahead. He still has a remnant, and we should be manifesting the banners of His tribe. Again, this is figurative, but it is also literal. God prepared the Sons of Israel with camps on the four corners, a type of the Cross, under literal flags.

Ultimately, there is one underlying point to both warfare and using banners in both our warfare and our worship. It's a point Jesus makes in John:

And I, when I am lifted up from the earth, will draw all people to myself." (John 12:32)

Flags, banners, and the related tools of worship aren't appendages we use because they look nice, but they are natural extensions. From establishing camps, to overcoming the enemy, to worship in celebration and dance, the Lord Himself has presented these tools of worship to us throughout His word as a normal and natural extension of worship and a reflection of the ultimate act of worship.

Literally, we see the Cross as a banner of warfare itself. But it is a concept that should continue today. When we lift Him up, not only in the traditional ways in our worship, but also with dance and flags, banners, streamers, when it's with a heart for Him and His kingdom, it will, by His anointing, draw people to Him.

Chapter Four

Prophecy and intercession in worship dance

For the testimony of Jesus is the spirit of prophecy-

-Revelation 19:10

Intercession and prophecy are powerful aspects of the Christian life, as well as of dance. It's almost unheard of that a Christian of any upbringing does not learn to pray on some level. Unfortunately, often the prayers stop at words. We teach people to come to an altar and say a pray to ask Jesus into their hearts. Then we tell them to pray for people to get saved, pray for the sick, and pray that God will help them get better. And the list goes on. It's no wonder to me, as a person who is easily bored, why people don't pray very much if that is all they think there is.

There is so much more, brothers and sisters, so much deeper and so much richer! Although the aforementioned is absolutely true, it doesn't always produce sustaining prayer. I have deep respect for those I have known in their 50s and 60s who have managed to discipline themselves and faithfully pray this way every day for decades. Make no mistake, prayer with a pure heart and in the will of God is *always* right. But few can *sustain* it this way, especially in a culture that is fast-paced and holds multitasking as a normative way of life.

To explore how prayer combines with dance, worship and warfare, let's look at what prayer is by the biblical definition.

The primary word we know as intercession is a Hebrew word which is a verb—an action word, not a noun!—is Strong's **H6293 pâga**, and it means:

A primitive root; to impinge, by accident or violence, or (figuratively) by importunity: - come (betwixt), cause to entreat, fall (upon), make intercession, intercessor, intreat, lay, light [upon], meet (together), pray, reach, run.

Now let's compare that to Webster's secular definition.

*In`ter*ces"sion\, n. [L. intercessio an intervention, a becoming surety: cf. F. intercession. See <u>Intercede</u>.] The act of interceding; mediation; interposition between parties at variance, with a view to reconciliation; prayer, petition, or entreaty in favor of, or (less often) against, another or others. Intercession. (n.d.). Webster's Revised Unabridged Dictionary. Retrieved*

September 26, 2008, from Dictionary.com website:
http://dictionary.reference.com/browse/intercession

Before we expand on that, I want to add another word to the mix: *Prophecy*. Prophecy gets a bad reputation sometimes today because of the "showy" prophets. A lot of people don't think of it as something directly associated with prayer, but it is. First the Strong's definition:

G4394 prophēteia, from G4396 *("prophecy"); prediction (scriptural or other): - prophecy, prophesying. (Strong's)*

And Webster's:

Proph"e*cy\, n.; pl. <u>*Prophecies,*</u>

1. A declaration of something to come; a foretelling; a prediction; esp., an inspired foretelling.

Prophecy came not in old time by the will of man. --2. Pet. i. 21.

2. (Script.) A book of prophecies; a history; as, the prophecy of Ahijah. --2 Chron. ix. 29.

3. Public interpretation of Scripture; preaching; exhortation or instruction.

Prophecy. (n.d.). Webster's Revised Unabridged Dictionary. Retrieved September 26, 2008, from Dictionary.com website: *http://dictionary.reference.com/browse/prophecy*

Combining these terms, you have the idea of what we call *prophetic intercession*, which expresses the heart of God, not our hearts. Often our own prayers go from our hearts to God. Prophetic prayers plant God's heart in our heart, which go *back* to God's heart.

Mike Bickle, of the International House of Prayer, jokes about how funny intercession itself is in a logical sense: "God, you're telling me to sit in a room and tell You what you're telling me? Couldn't I be out *doing* something?" Essentially, this is just a part of God's plan, his spiritual opposite to our natural logic.

If dance is a normal part of worship, as we discussed previously, then we can expect that it would incorporate prophecy and intercession as worship does. We see this in the ultimate worship service in Heaven in Revelation:

And when he had taken the scroll, the four living creatures and the twenty-four elders fell down before the Lamb, each holding a harp, and golden bowls full of incense, which are the prayers of the saints. (Revelation 5:8)

The "Harp and Bowl" model of worship, born out of this Scripture, has grown from the IHOP-KC prayer room in the Midwest to being a term many in the church use today to denote their own "style" of worship. However, it's clearly a biblical style that somehow got replaced with one-dimensional worship that was never intended to be the only way.

It's through this type of worship we sustain intercession. Dance is a part of this in its direct connection to regular worship. To pray for hours and hours isn't always easy for most; however, when we combine these elements, worship and intercession are mixed and sustained so we have the support, the drive, and the press to battle, and to fulfill the call to pray.

If we consider dance as a normal part of worship, which clearly we can do, we can also expect that prophecy would be an aspect. From 1 Chronicles, where David establishes a prophetic worship ministry (see chapters 15, 16 and 25) until Revelation, we see prophetic ministry as a norm in Scriptural worship.

A key Scripture on prophecy and what it is can be found in Revelation:

Then I fell down at his feet to worship him, but he said to me, "You must not do that! I am a fellow servant with you and your brothers who hold to the testimony of Jesus. Worship God." For the testimony of Jesus is the spirit of prophecy. (Rev 19:10)

The word testimony is **G3141: *marturia G3144;*** *evidence given (judicially or generally): - record, report, testimony, witness.* Adding to this are Jesus' own words in John 16:

When the Spirit of truth comes, he will guide you into all the truth, for he will not speak on his own authority, but whatever he hears he will speak, and he will declare to you the things that are to come. He will glorify me, for he will take what is mine and declare it to you. All that the Father has is mine; therefore I said that he will take what is mine and declare it to you. (John 16:13-15)

Jesus actually tells us that the Holy Spirit will reveal the Father's heart to us, that the Spirit will declare to us the things that are to come. It's a rather astonishing statement to grasp in our human minds, that the Holy Spirit, a real person who lives inside each believer, would speak to us, as He did Jesus on earth, and tell us those things. But that is exactly what He does. Think about the implications of this statement in light of Revelation 19:10 (above) and intercession and prophecy in general.

Of course, Paul teaches on prophecy in 1 Corinthians over the course of three chapters (1 Corinthians 12-14), as he discusses the gifts of the Spirit and the importance of love in their operation. Let's look at his take on prophecy itself (which should never be taken separate from 1 Corinthians 13 on love, as that is the basis for the use of all spiritual gifts, as well as the intended outcome of their use):

Pursue love, and earnestly desire the spiritual gifts, especially that you may prophesy. (2) For one who speaks in a tongue speaks not to men but to God; for no one understands him, but he utters mysteries in the Spirit. (3) On the other hand, the one who prophesies speaks to people for their upbuilding and encouragement and consolation. (4) The one who speaks in a tongue builds up himself, but the one who prophesies builds up the church. (5) Now I want you all to speak in tongues,

but even more to prophesy. The one who prophesies is greater than the one who speaks in tongues, unless someone interprets, so that the church may be built up. (1Cor 14:1-5)

And of course, Amos makes a bold statement we often disregard:

For the Lord GOD does nothing without revealing his secret to his servants the prophets. (Amos 3:7)

We often reduce prophecy to a one-dimensional prediction for a person, which sometimes is really God's heart and (let's be honest) sometimes isn't. But true prophecy is forth-telling—it's filled with dimension. The prophetic heart of God can be danced. Witness, for example, if God were speaking to a church body regarding its need to revive itself, its lacking of passion. Picture how a prophetic dance would "show not tell" this concept. To see the passion come alive under the genuine anointing of God, to stir hearts with emotion, is probably going to result in more of a prophetic impact than a person calling out "the Lord says..." from the back of the church. While both can be entirely valid forms of prophecy, God is a creative artist. He isn't limited, but we often limit ourselves and who we think He is in relation to us.

Creativity is a key in the premises put forth in this study. God is creative. Period. Genesis proves this, even without the rest of the Bible. God who made the mind and heart, the earth and heaven, male and female, that same God doesn't do everything one way. We may! We may find a way that works and pursue it as *the* way, but it's probably not. Scripture has absolutes, but they are in morality, holy living, doing justice, among others, not in expressions of worship and love for God. It is a pharisaical attitude that declares God wouldn't do it this way. He would and He does. That isn't to say there aren't those who "taint" it, but those are people issues, not God ones. I usually dislike clichés, but this one, which is so often used in dance ministry comments, is true—

we cannot "throw the baby out with the bathwater." So we return to a key verse in all of our study:

And I, when I am lifted up from the earth, will draw all people to myself. (John 12:32)

God uses dance, as He does all forms of worship, to draw us to Him, to exalt His name, and to execute His decrees. The Old Testament gives us a foundation for this in various instances. Carefully examine these passages:

Then Miriam the prophetess, the sister of Aaron, took a tambourine in her hand, and all the women went out after her with tambourines and dancing. (21) And Miriam sang to them: "Sing to the LORD, for he has triumphed gloriously; the horse and his rider he has thrown into the sea." (Exodus 15:20-21)

And it came to pass, when the evil spirit from God was upon Saul, that David took the harp, and played with his hand: so Saul was refreshed, and was well, and the evil spirit departed from him. (1Samuel 16:23)

As they were coming home, when David returned from striking down the Philistine, the women came out of all the cities of Israel, singing and dancing, to meet King Saul, with tambourines, with songs of joy, and with musical instruments. (7) And the women sang to one another as they celebrated, "Saul has struck down his thousands, and David his ten thousands." (8) And Saul was very angry, and this saying displeased him. He said, "They have ascribed to David ten thousands, and to me they have ascribed thousands, and what more can he have but the kingdom?" (9) And Saul eyed David from that day on. (10) The next day a harmful spirit from God rushed upon Saul, and he raved within his house while David was playing the lyre, as he did day by day. Saul had his spear in his hand. (11) And Saul hurled the spear, for he thought, "I will pin David to the wall." But David evaded him twice. (12) Saul was afraid of David because the LORD was with him but had departed from Saul. (13)

So Saul removed him from his presence and made him a commander of a thousand. And he went out and came in before the people. (14) And David had success in all his undertakings, for the LORD was with him. (I Samuel 18:6-14)

Remember David and the Ark of the Covenant? This reminds us of both the importance of worship, but also of keeping it in the honor and reverence of God's holiness:

(2)And David arose and went with all the people who were with him from Baale-judah to bring up from there the ark of God, which is called by the name of the LORD of hosts who sits enthroned on the cherubim.... (5) And David and all the house of Israel were making merry before the LORD, with songs and lyres and harps and tambourines and castanets and cymbals. (6) And when they came to the threshing floor of Nacon, Uzzah put out his hand to the ark of God and took hold of it, for the oxen stumbled. (7) And the anger of the LORD was kindled against Uzzah, and God struck him down there because of his error, and he died there beside the ark of God. (8) And David was angry because the LORD had burst forth against Uzzah. And that place is called Perez-uzzah, to this day. (9) And David was afraid of the LORD that day, and he said, "How can the ark of the LORD come to me?" (10) So David was not willing to take the ark of the LORD into the city of David. But David took it aside to the house of Obed-edom the Gittite. (11) And the ark of the LORD remained in the house of Obed-edom the Gittite three months, and the LORD blessed Obed-edom and all his household. (12) And it was told King David, "The LORD has blessed the household of Obed-edom and all that belongs to him, because of the ark of God." So David went and brought up the ark of God from the house of Obed-edom to the city of David with rejoicing... (14) And David danced before the LORD with all his might. And David was wearing a linen ephod. (15) So David and all the house of Israel brought up the ark of the LORD with shouting and with the sound of the horn. (16) As the ark of the LORD came into the city of David, Michal the daughter of Saul looked out of the window and saw King David leaping and dancing before the LORD, and she despised him in her heart. (17) And they brought in the ark of the LORD and set it in its place, inside the tent that David had pitched for it. And David offered burnt offerings and peace offerings before the LORD.... (20) And David returned to bless his household. But Michal the daughter of Saul came out to meet David and said, "How the king of Israel honored himself today, uncovering himself today before the eyes of his servants' female servants, as one of the vulgar fellows shamelessly uncovers himself!" (21) And David said to Michal, "It was before the LORD, who chose me above your father and above all his house, to appoint me as prince over Israel, the people of the LORD--and I will make merry before the LORD. (22) I will make myself yet more contemptible than this, and I will be abased in your eyes. But by the female servants of whom you have spoken, by them I shall be held in honor." (23) And Michal the daughter of Saul had no child to the day of her death. (2 Samuel 6; refs listed above) (See also 1 Chron. 15: 1-17, 20-23)

Say also: "Save us, O God of our salvation, and gather and deliver us from among the nations, that we may give thanks to your holy name, and glory in your praise. (36) Blessed be the LORD, the God of Israel, from everlasting to everlasting!" Then all the people said, "Amen!" and praised the LORD. (37) So David left Asaph and his brothers there before the ark of the covenant of the LORD to minister regularly before the ark as each day required, (38) and also Obed-edom and his sixty-eight brothers, while Obed-edom, the son of Jeduthun, and Hosah were to be gatekeepers. (39) And he left Zadok the priest and his brothers the priests before the tabernacle of the LORD in the high place that was at Gibeon (40) to offer burnt offerings to the LORD on the altar of burnt offering regularly morning and evening, to do all that is written in the Law of the LORD that he commanded Israel. (41) With them were Heman and Jeduthun and the rest of those chosen and expressly named to give thanks to the LORD, for his steadfast love endures forever. (42) Heman and Jeduthun had trumpets and cymbals for the music and instruments for sacred song. The sons of Jeduthun were appointed to the gate. (43) Then all the people departed each to his house, and David went home to bless his household. (I Chronicles 16:35-43)

Prophetic Dance in Spiritual Warfare

Prophetic dance often expresses in a physical form what we see spiritually, as we have examined before, and it provides further exercise of spiritual warfare. Often we discern things or know things from the heart of God that need an act of warfare.

Though an army encamp against me, my heart shall not fear; though war arise against me, yet I will be confident. (Psalm 27:3)

Remember that the powers and principalities of darkness are literal and real and are actually living in the air around us:

For we do not wrestle against flesh and blood, but against the rulers, against the authorities, against the cosmic powers over this present darkness, against the spiritual forces of evil in the heavenly places. (Ephesians 6:12)

When we dance not simply out of worship (which is obviously important and good), but in response to what we are hearing from God, it is a prophetic act that can move spiritual forces of evil. Likewise, when we pray in this manner, praying the heart of God, it serves as a *pâga* encounter right there in the dance—a literal dance of intercession, meeting with God and hearing His heart.

These instances will often cause the Spirit of God to move in us in a greater measure. It's a myth that we have to only stand up and yell "thus saith the Lord" to operate prophetically. God is creative and innovative; He doesn't need our yelling and spiritual language. He needs our hearts of worship and love toward Him.

As a writing teacher, one principle I try to impart to my students is "show, don't tell." It's a key in good writing, and it has application here. While certainly God does "tell," I have seen the element of creative expression often be more effective in a modern generation. The issue, of course, is a cultural one. God and His Word do not change, yet God is a wise Father who knows that in the case of an artistic young man or a cynical young lady, a person who has been injured by "thus saith the Lord" (when sometimes He didn't), and other blocks we often have, that His message can reach people in various ways. A dance expressing the heart of God, a literal march with flags, or banners in motion, can bring the "show" aspect to the "tell" arena and work together to strengthen the message. The bottom line is never our perception, but the Word of God. Does the creative expression match the Word? Does it testify about Jesus? Does it lift up His name? These should be our concerns; when we focus on Jesus, the other avenues tend to fall into place.

Prophetic intercession is displayed in a group worship setting in I Samuel:

After that you shall come to Gibeath-elohim, where there is a garrison of the Philistines. And there, as soon as you come to the city, you will meet a group of prophets coming down from the high place with harp, tambourine, flute, and lyre before them, prophesying. (6) Then the Spirit of the LORD will rush upon you, and you will prophesy with them and be turned into another man. (7) Now when these signs meet you, do what your hand finds to do, for God is with you. (8) Then go down before me to Gilgal. And behold, I am coming to you to offer burnt offerings and to sacrifice peace offerings. Seven days you shall wait, until I come to you and show you what you shall do." (9) When he turned his back to leave Samuel, God gave him another heart. And all these signs came to

pass that day. (10) When they came to Gibeah, behold, a group of prophets met him, and the Spirit of God rushed upon him, and he prophesied among them. (11) And when all who knew him previously saw how he prophesied with the prophets, the people said to one another, "What has come over the son of Kish? Is Saul also among the prophets?" (12) And a man of the place answered, "And who is their father?" Therefore it became a proverb, "Is Saul also among the prophets?" (13) When he had finished prophesying, he came to the high place. (1 Samuel 10:5 -13)

Also look at this:

David and the chiefs of the service also set apart for the service the sons of Asaph, and of Heman, and of Jeduthun, who prophesied with lyres, with harps, and with cymbals. (1 Chronicles 25:1)

Some don't equate musical instruments with worship tools like flags; however, they are used interchangeably in the Bible in many instances. A tambourine functions as an instrumental weapon of warfare alongside banners. Armies in the Bible march with instruments, singers, and banners all at once. So passages like the following would seem silly if we said, "well, they can march with those instruments but not a flag." The fact is, even high school marching bands have flag corps. The world has already grasped what we sometimes debate.

And once again, I must emphasize parts of Psalm 149 here, which we have already looked at as a whole:

(3) Let them praise his name with dancing, making melody to him with tambourine and lyre! (6)Let the high praises of God be in their throats and two-edged swords in their hands, (7)to execute vengeance on the nations and punishments on the peoples, (8)to bind their kings with chains and their nobles with fetters of iron, (9) to execute on them the judgment written! This is honor for all his godly ones. Praise the LORD! (v. 3, 6-9)

Chapter Five

Celebration in worship dance

Praise him with tambourine and dance....

let everything that has breath

praise the LORD!

-Psalm 150: 4, 6

If you have had experience with worship dance, chances are celebrative dance was your first, maybe only style. It is much like that day I first danced, when the song of celebration and rejoicing in the Lord was played, and my feet left the ground in new freedom. But just as it was a miraculous turn for me, celebration in dance is not just a good time. It's an act of worship and thanksgiving.

Praise the LORD! Praise God in his sanctuary; praise him in his mighty heavens! (2) Praise him for his mighty deeds; praise him according to his excellent greatness! (3) Praise him with trumpet sound; praise him with lute and harp! (4) Praise him with tambourine and dance; praise him with strings and pipe! (5) Praise him with sounding cymbals; praise him with loud clashing cymbals! (6) Let everything that has breath praise the LORD! Praise the LORD! (Psalm 150: 1-6)

Psalm 150 shares some similar themes with Psalm 149, as well. The power of the warfare and praise, and the execution of powerful praise is a prevalent theme throughout the word of God, and some of the words in the original language are surprising. We read them now, in our translations, as words that mean "happy" things, but as we will see, sometimes what they really mean, in a literal sense, is dance.

And you shall take on the first day the fruit of splendid trees, branches of palm trees and boughs of leafy trees and willows of the brook, and you shall rejoice before the LORD your God seven days. (Leviticus 23:40)

If you have seen traditional Jewish dancing you probably have noticed dances in the round and lots of celebration. In fact, Lucinda Coleman says in her article "Worship God in Dance," that "in the Hebrew tradition, dance functioned as a medium of prayer and praise, as an expression of joy and reverence, and as a mediator between God and humanity" (Taylor 1976:81, qtd. in Coleman).

Celebrative dance occurs as the result of the goodness of God. While dance is often considered something "special," if we look at both the history of the reactions of the works of God, as well as an uninhibited person's natural reaction (think about how children react), we can see it is entirely common to react to the goodness of God with movement and dance.

Now Peter and John were going up to the temple at the hour of prayer, the ninth hour. (2) And a man lame from birth was being carried, whom they laid daily at the gate of the temple that is called the Beautiful Gate to ask alms of those entering the temple. (3) Seeing Peter and John about to go into the temple, he asked to receive alms. (4) And Peter directed his gaze at him, as did John, and said, "Look at us." (5) And he fixed his attention on them, expecting to receive something from them. (6) But Peter said, "I have no silver and gold, but what I do have I give to you. In the name of Jesus Christ of Nazareth, rise up and walk!" (7) And he took him by the right hand and raised him up, and immediately his feet and ankles were made strong. (8) And leaping up he stood and began to walk, and entered the temple with them, walking and leaping and praising God. (9) And all the people saw him walking and praising God, (10) and recognized him as the one who sat at the Beautiful Gate of the temple, asking for alms. And they were filled with wonder and amazement at what had happened to him. (Act 3:1-10)

Stop for a minute and picture what this might have looked like. If a man who could not walk was now "walking and leaping and praising God," do you think, perhaps, it would look a little wild to the human eye?

Or would we say it was not wild because of his lifetime of being lame? Is it okay for the sick to rejoice in wild celebration? And if it is, aren't we all the "sick" without Jesus. Remember what Jesus says to the church at Philadelphia:

"I know your works. Behold, I have set before you an open door, which no one is able to shut. I know that you have but little power, and yet you have kept my word and have not denied my name. (11) I am coming soon. Hold fast what you have, so that no one may seize your crown." (Revelation 3:8, 11)

He tells them to stay strong, pursue maturity. He doesn't say that since they are saved and truly love Him, they are okay, but He tells them to "hold fast." So if we were set free, redeemed, delivered, made victorious, healed, saved, should we ever stop celebrating? Is a time of celebrative worship not a time for us to enter in and reflect with rejoicing at what we have? Holding fast means pursuing continually, not that we once pursued and might again.

The Bible shows us many instances of those who rejoice and celebrate in the dance:

1Sa 29:5 - Is not this David, of whom they sing to one another in dances, 'Saul has struck down his thousands, and David his ten thousands'?

Deu 16:11 - And you shall rejoice before the LORD your God, you and your son and your daughter, your male servant and your female servant, the Levite who is within your towns, the sojourner, the fatherless, and the widow who are among you, at the place that the LORD your God will choose, to make his name dwell there.

To celebrate is also to rejoice: Strong's **H1523** *primitive root; properly to spin around (under the influence of any violent emotion), that is, usually rejoice, or (as cringing) fear: - be glad, joy, be joyful, rejoice.*

In the following Scriptures the Hebrew root is *1523*, showing dance is a natural response. (This is the same Strong's number as the passage in Zephaniah 3:17 which tells us God rejoices over us with singing.)

1Ch 16:31 - Let the heavens be glad, and let the earth rejoice, and let them say among the nations, "The LORD reigns!"

Psa 2:11 - Serve the LORD with fear, and rejoice with trembling.

Psa 9:14 - That I may recount all your praises, that in the gates of the daughter of Zion I may rejoice in your salvation.

Psa 89:15-16 - Blessed are the people who know the festal shout, who walk, O LORD, in the light of your face, who exult in your name all the day and in your righteousness are exalted.

Psa 21:1 - O LORD, in your strength the king rejoices, and in your salvation how greatly he exults!

Pro 23:24-25 - The father of the righteous will greatly rejoice; he who fathers a wise son will be glad in him. Let your father and mother be glad; let her who bore you rejoice.

Isa 9:3 - You have multiplied the nation; you have increased its joy; they rejoice before you as with joy at the harvest, as they are glad when they divide the spoil.

Isa 41:15-16 - Behold, I make of you a threshing sledge, new, sharp, and having teeth; you shall thresh the mountains and crush them, and you shall make the hills like chaff; you shall winnow them, and the wind shall carry them away, and the tempest shall scatter them. And you shall rejoice in the LORD; in the Holy One of Israel you shall glory.

Isa 29:19 - The meek shall obtain fresh joy in the LORD, and the poor among mankind shall exult in the Holy One of Israel.

Psa 16:9 - Therefore my heart is glad, and my whole being rejoices; my flesh also dwells secure.

Isa 61:10 - I will greatly rejoice in the LORD; my soul shall exult in my God, for he has clothed me with the garments of salvation; he has covered me with the robe of righteousness, as a bridegroom decks himself like a priest with a beautiful headdress, and as a bride adorns herself with her jewels.

Zec 10:7 - Then Ephraim shall become like a mighty warrior, and their hearts shall be glad as with wine. Their children shall see it and be glad; their hearts shall rejoice in the LORD.

<u>Celebration Connected with the Prophetic</u>

We respond, much of the time, to the Word of God with celebration and rejoicing. Prophecy is a forth-telling, a foreknowledge of what God is doing or going to do (see last chapter for more explanation). With that in mind, it's pretty clear we would respond to much genuine prophecy of the acts of God with celebration. While it seems logical that we would only respond this way in "happy" words, we should remember that even His judgments on sin are a step closer to our inheritance, and we should desire to respond out of a pure heart aligned with God, and to join Him in rejecting sin.

Miriam rejoices in dance at the victory in Exodus 15, where God is declared **"The LORD is a man of war; the LORD is his name"** (v. 3) who executes justice on their enemies and delvers them:

Then Miriam the prophetess, the sister of Aaron, took a tambourine in her hand, and all the women went out after her with tambourines and dancing. (21) And Miriam sang to them: "Sing to the LORD, for he has triumphed gloriously; the horse and his rider he has thrown into the sea." (Exodus 15:20-21)

Joel 2 is known as a sober and intense passage speaking of the day of the Lord, and yet it says to rejoice, not at the calamity, but at the justice of a righteous God:

Be glad, O children of Zion, and rejoice in the LORD your God, for he has given the early rain for your vindication; he has poured down for you abundant rain, the early and the latter rain, as before. (24) The threshing floors shall be full of grain; the vats shall overflow with wine and oil. (25) I will restore to you the years that the swarming locust has eaten, the hopper, the destroyer, and the cutter, my great army, which I sent among you. (26) You shall eat in plenty and be satisfied, and praise the name of the LORD your God, who has dealt wondrously with you. And my people shall never again be put to shame. (27) You shall know that I am in the midst of Israel, and that I am the LORD your God and there is none else. And my people shall never again be put to shame. (28) And it shall come to pass afterward, that I will pour out my Spirit on all flesh; your sons and your daughters shall prophesy, your old men shall dream dreams, and your young men shall see visions. (29) Even on the male and female servants in those days I will pour out my Spirit. (30) And I will show wonders in the heavens and on the earth, blood and fire and columns of smoke. (31) The sun shall be turned to darkness, and the moon to blood, before the great and awesome day of the LORD comes. (32) And it shall come to pass that everyone who calls on the name of the LORD shall be saved. For in Mount Zion and in Jerusalem there shall be those who escape, as the LORD has said, and among the survivors shall be those whom the LORD calls. (Joel 2:23-32)**

Celebration is Spiritual Warfare

At the risk of sounding redundant, Ephesians 6:11-18 still applies even in celebration—read it again, reflecting on the celebrative aspects we are discussing and see how that affects your application in this context:

Put on the whole armor of God, that you may be able to stand against the schemes of the devil. (12) For we do not wrestle against flesh and blood, but against the rulers, against the authorities, against the cosmic powers over

this present darkness, against the spiritual forces of evil in the heavenly places. (13) Therefore take up the whole armor of God, that you may be able to withstand in the evil day, and having done all, to stand firm. (14) Stand therefore, having fastened on the belt of truth, and having put on the breastplate of righteousness, (15) and, as shoes for your feet, having put on the readiness given by the gospel of peace. (16) In all circumstances take up the shield of faith, with which you can extinguish all the flaming darts of the evil one; (17) and take the helmet of salvation, and the sword of the Spirit, which is the word of God, (18) praying at all times in the Spirit, with all prayer and supplication. To that end keep alert with all perseverance, making supplication for all the saints (Ephesians 6:11-18)

It is an act of spiritual warfare to rejoice in despair, to celebrate a victory not yet seen, to literally call those things that are not as though they are. Romans says:

That is why it depends on faith, in order that the promise may rest on grace and be guaranteed to all his offspring-- not only to the adherent of the law but also to the one who shares the faith of Abraham, who is the father of us all, (17) as it is written, "I have made you the father of many nations"--in the presence of the God in whom he believed, who gives life to the dead and calls into existence the things that do not exist. (Rom 4:16-17)

Rejoice for what is to come:

Zec 9:9 - Rejoice greatly, O daughter of Zion! Shout aloud, O daughter of Jerusalem! Behold, your king is coming to you; righteous and having salvation is he, humble and mounted on a donkey, on a colt, the foal of a donkey.

Isa 65:18-19 - But be glad and rejoice forever in that which I create; for behold, I create Jerusalem to be a joy, and her people to be a gladness. I will rejoice in Jerusalem and be glad in my people; no more shall be heard in it the sound of weeping and the cry of distress.

Psa 51:8 - Let me hear joy and gladness; let the bones that you have broken rejoice.

Zep 3:17 - The LORD your God is in your midst, a mighty one who will save; he will rejoice over you with gladness; he will quiet you by his love; he will exult over you with loud singing. *(*Exult *is the word translated to mean what we would call "dance" in this passage—Strong's H1523.)*

We Celebrate Healing in Dance

Psalm 30 is a well-known description of rejoicing at God's healing and delivering powers:

I will extol you, O LORD, for you have drawn me up and have not let my foes rejoice over me. (2) O LORD my God, I cried to you for help, and you have healed me. (3) O LORD, you have brought up my soul from Sheol; you restored me to life from among those who go down to the pit. (4) Sing praises to the LORD, O you his saints, and give thanks to his holy name. (5) For his anger is but for a moment, and his favor is for a lifetime. Weeping may tarry for the night, but joy comes with the morning. (6) As for me, I said in my prosperity, "I shall never be moved." (7) By your favor, O LORD, you made my mountain stand strong; you hid your face; I was dismayed. (8) To you, O LORD, I cry, and to the Lord I plead for mercy: (9) "What profit is there in my death, if I go down to the pit? Will the dust praise you? Will it tell of your faithfulness? (10) Hear, O LORD, and be merciful to me! O LORD, be my helper!" (11) You have turned for me my mourning into dancing; you have loosed my sackcloth and clothed me with gladness, (12) that my glory may sing your praise and not be silent. O LORD my God, I will give thanks to you forever! (Psalm 30:1-12)

Each of the following Scriptures refers to Strong's word *H2342, chûl/chîyl,* which means: *properly to spin around (under the influence of any violent emotion), that is, usually rejoice, or (as cringing) fear: - be glad, joy, be joyful, rejoice.*

Psa 14:7 - Oh, that salvation for Israel would come out of Zion! When the LORD restores the fortunes of his people, let Jacob rejoice, let Israel be glad.

Isa 49:13 - Sing for joy, O heavens, and exult, O earth; break forth, O mountains, into singing! For the LORD has comforted his people and will have compassion on his afflicted.

Psa 53:6 - Oh, that salvation for Israel would come out of Zion! When God restores the fortunes of his people, let Jacob rejoice, let Israel be glad.

Psa 31:7 - I will rejoice and be glad in your steadfast love, because you have seen my affliction; you have known the distress of my soul.

This spinning, dancing, rejoicing, even where it appears "wild" is shown as appropriate, normal, and good to respond to healing, whether manifested or to come, with dancing in celebration for the healing power of God.

Chapter Six

The processional

Your procession is seen, O God,

the procession of my God, my King,

into the sanctuary

-Psalm 68:24

T he processional type of dance serves as a corporate exercise of a deliberate act of war, celebration or other spiritual endeavor, often combining at least some of the methods already discussed in this book.

The Bible speaks about processionals, as well:

Your procession is seen, O God, the procession of my God, my King, into the sanctuary-(25) the singers in front, the musicians last, between them virgins playing tambourines: (26) "Bless God in the great congregation, the LORD, O you who are of Israel's fountain!"(Psalm 68:24-26)

The next day the large crowd that had come to the feast heard that Jesus was coming to Jerusalem. (13) So they took branches of palm trees and went out to meet him, crying out, "Hosanna! Blessed is he who comes in the name of the Lord, even the King of Israel!" (John 12:12-13)

The processional serves as a unified advancement in the name and authority of God. The word for processional in Psalm 68 is **Strong's H1979**, translated *goings* in the KJV: *a walking; by implication a procession or march, a caravan: - company, going, walk, way.*

Other meanings of procession in the Bible:

H2287, chagag: *A primitive root (compare H2283, H2328); properly to move in a circle, that is, (specifically) to march in a sacred procession, to observe a festival; by implication to be giddy: - celebrate, dance, (keep, hold) a (solemn) feast (holiday), reel to and fro.*

G2358, thriambeuo: *From a prolonged compound of the base of G2360 and a derivative of G680 (meaning a noisy iambus, sung in honor of Bacchus); to make an acclamatory procession, that is, (figuratively) to conquer or (by Hebraism) to give victory: - (cause) to triumph (over).*

Consider the implications of a unified front as a church body:

Deu 32:30 - How could one have chased a thousand, and two have put ten thousand to flight, unless their Rock had sold them, and the LORD had given them up?

Psa 42:4 - These things I remember, as I pour out my soul: how I would go with the throng and lead them in procession to the house of God with glad shouts and songs of praise, a multitude keeping festival.

Mat 18:20 - For where two or three are gathered in my name, there am I among them.

Processionals have a natural opposite, just as most spiritual things do. Consider these: The circus processional, bridal processionals (which are actually called processionals), military processionals, and Olympic processionals; even protest marches are a type of processionals.

God Himself initiates this advancement. Processionals are ordained by God. It was the LORD who told Joshua how to take the city by using, literally, a processional:

You shall march around the city, all the men of war going around the city once. Thus shall you do for six days (4) Seven priests shall bear seven trumpets of rams' horns before the ark. On the seventh day you shall march around the city seven times, and the priests shall blow the trumpets.(5) And when they make a long blast with the ram's horn, when you hear the sound of the trumpet, then all the people shall shout with a great shout, and the wall of the city will fall down flat, and the people shall go up, everyone straight before him." (6) So Joshua the son of Nun called the priests and said to them, "Take up the ark of the covenant and let seven priests bear seven trumpets of rams' horns before the ark of the LORD." (7) And he said to the people, "Go forward. March around the city and let the armed men pass on before the ark of the LORD." (8) And just as Joshua had commanded the people, the seven priests bearing the seven trumpets of rams' horns before the LORD went forward, blowing the trumpets, with the ark of the covenant of the LORD

following them. (9) The armed men were walking before the priests who were blowing the trumpets, and the rear guard was walking after the ark, while the trumpets blew continually. (10) But Joshua commanded the people, "You shall not shout or make your voice heard, neither shall any word go out of your mouth, until the day I tell you to shout. Then you shall shout." (11) So he caused the ark of the LORD to circle the city, going about it once. And they came into the camp and spent the night in the camp. (12) Then Joshua rose early in the morning, and the priests took up the ark of the LORD. (13) And the seven priests bearing the seven trumpets of rams' horns before the ark of the LORD walked on, and they blew the trumpets continually. And the armed men were walking before them, and the rear guard was walking after the ark of the LORD, while the trumpets blew continually. (14) And the second day they marched around the city once, and returned into the camp. So they did for six days. (15) On the seventh day they rose early, at the dawn of day, and marched around the city in the same manner seven times. It was only on that day that they marched around the city seven times. (16) And at the seventh time, when the priests had blown the trumpets, Joshua said to the people, "Shout, for the LORD has given you the city. (17) And the city and all that is within it shall be devoted to the LORD for destruction. Only Rahab the prostitute and all who are with her in her house shall live, because she hid the messengers whom we sent. (18) But you, keep yourselves from the things devoted to destruction, lest when you have devoted them you take any of the devoted things and make the camp of Israel a thing for destruction and bring trouble upon it. (19) But all silver and gold, and every vessel of bronze and iron, are holy to the LORD; they shall go into the treasury of the LORD."(20) So the people shouted, and the trumpets were blown. As soon as the people heard the sound of the trumpet, the people shouted a great shout, and the wall fell down flat, so that the people went up into the city, every man straight before him, and they captured the city. (Joshua 6:3-20)

Processionals are an aspect of effective spiritual warfare. This pattern is shown throughout the Bible. A notable example of this occurs with Jehoshaphat:

And they rose early in the morning and went out into the wilderness of Tekoa. And when they went out, Jehoshaphat stood and said, "Hear me, Judah and inhabitants of Jerusalem! Believe in the LORD your God, and you will be established; believe his prophets, and you will succeed." (21) And when he had taken counsel with the people, he appointed those who were to sing to the LORD and praise him in holy attire, as they went before the army, and say, "Give thanks to the LORD, for his steadfast love endures forever." (22) And when they began to sing and praise, the LORD set an ambush against the men of Ammon, Moab, and Mount Seir, who had come against Judah, so that they were routed. (23) For the men of Ammon and Moab rose against the inhabitants of Mount Seir, devoting them to destruction, and when they had made an end of the inhabitants of Seir, they all helped to destroy one another. (24) When Judah came to the watchtower of the wilderness, they looked toward the horde, and behold, there were dead bodies lying on the ground; none had escaped. (25) When Jehoshaphat and his people came to take their spoil, they found among them, in great numbers, goods, clothing, and precious things, which they took for themselves until they could carry no more. They were three days in taking the spoil, it was so much. (26) On the fourth day they assembled in the Valley of Beracah, for there they blessed the LORD. Therefore the name of that place has been called the Valley of Beracah to this day. (27) Then they returned, every man of Judah and Jerusalem, and Jehoshaphat at their head, returning to Jerusalem with joy, for the LORD had made them rejoice over their enemies. (28) They came to Jerusalem with harps and

lyres and trumpets, to the house of the LORD. (29) And the fear of God came on all the kingdoms of the countries when they heard that the LORD had fought against the enemies of Israel. (30) So the realm of Jehoshaphat was quiet, for his God gave him rest all around. (2 Chronicles 20:20-30)

Once again we cannot ignore the elements of the armor of God presented in Ephesians 6. What better demonstration on the use of the body in spiritual warfare, celebration, and worship? These elements, clearly, are what we see in processionals as well.

Processionals are not necessarily choreographed productions. The unchoreographed processional occurs when freedom, intercession, celebration, or war break forth from a unified people, but in individual demonstrations which still operate in unity. We have seen this throughout several examples of warfare and celebration, as well. Processionals are often a mix of dance types and styles, and they tend to include a variety of worship styles. In the Old Testament, as we have seen, a processional would often include tambourines, lyres, trumpets, dancing, leaping, and probably almost any other type of movement we can imagine.

It stands to reason that one type of dance is not used for every need. Imagine the secular processionals we have discussed and their variety of uses. Do we not have a similar application spiritually?

A processional may even include a mix of choreographed dances and unchoreographed dances to achieve the overall effect, message, or purpose.

When Jesus returns, we will see and *participate* in the ultimate processional. The book of Revelation details many processionals around the throne of God. Recall the earlier reference to the 12 tribes of Israel—their worship with the palm branches we already looked at is also a processional:

And I heard the number of the sealed, 144,000, sealed from every tribe of the sons of Israel: (5)12,000 from the

tribe of Judah were sealed, 12,000 from the tribe of Reuben, 12,000 from the tribe of Gad, (6) 12,000 from the tribe of Asher, 12,000 from the tribe of Naphtali, 12,000 from the tribe of Manasseh, (7) 12,000 from the tribe of Simeon, 12,000 from the tribe of Levi, 12,000 from the tribe of Issachar, (8) 12,000 from the tribe of Zebulun, 12,000 from the tribe of Joseph, 12,000 from the tribe of Benjamin were sealed. (9) After this I looked, and behold, a great multitude that no one could number, from every nation, from all tribes and peoples and languages, standing before the throne and before the Lamb, clothed in white robes, with palm branches in their hands, (10) and crying out with a loud voice, "Salvation belongs to our God who sits on the throne, and to the Lamb!" (11) And all the angels were standing around the throne and around the elders and the four living creatures, and they fell on their faces before the throne and worshiped God, (12) saying, "Amen! Blessing and glory and wisdom and thanksgiving and honor and power and might be to our God forever and ever! Amen." (Revelation 7:4-12)

While it doesn't say here they were marching in a processional, it's clear this is a type of processional, as the multitudes from all the nations and tribes stand before the throne of God with their palm branches worshiping the Lord.

Revelation details our ultimate and ongoing (eternal) processionals of worship before the glorious throne of God. Return to the picture of an Olympic processional, as all the nations enter in unity to begin the games, and magnify that picture as the flags of nations become the flag of the Lamb, and we enter in unity to worship the King of kings and the Lord of lords. This is what *awesome* looks like!

And they sing the song of Moses, the servant of God, and the song of the Lamb, saying, "Great and amazing are your deeds, O Lord God the Almighty! Just and true are your ways, O King of the nations! (4) Who will not fear, O Lord, and glorify your name? For you alone are holy. All

nations will come and worship you, for your righteous acts have been revealed." (Revelation 15:3-4)

And that is the key of David, the key that opens the doors in the spiritual realm that no person can shut, and shuts the doors in that same realm that no person can open. The spiritual and the natural parallel. What we do in the spiritual realm affects the natural realm.

The key of David is our key to victory:

And to the angel of the church in Philadelphia write: 'The words of the holy one, the true one, who has the key of David, who opens and no one will shut, who shuts and no one opens. I know your works. Behold, I have set before you an open door, which no one is able to shut. I know that you have but little power, and yet you have kept my word and have not denied my name. (Revelation 3:7-8)

Appendix

Further study on dance can be found through Shachah Ministries International:

www.shachah.org

Additional recommended books:

Restoring the Dance: Seeking God's Order

Anne Stevenson

My Body Is The Temple

Stephanie Butler

Further study on prayer and prophecy can be found through The International House of Prayer in Kansas City:

www.ihop.org

Additional recommended books:

Growing in the Prophetic

Mike Bickle

After God's Own Heart

Mike Bickle

Manufactured by Amazon.ca
Acheson, AB